KRISIT

Y York

BROADWAY PLAY PUBLISHING INC
New York
www.broadwayplaypublishing.com
info@broadwayplaypublishing.com

KRISIT

© Copyright 2001 Y York

First published by B P P I in October 2001 in *Plays By Y York, Volume 2*
First edition: July 2019
I S B N: 978-0-88145-800-8

Book design: Marie Donovan
Page make-up: Adobe InDesign
Typeface: Palatino

for Dad

KRISIT was originally commissioned by A Contemporary Theater. Subsequent workshops were at A Contemporary Theater (directed by Mark Lutwak) and San Jose Repertory Theater (Timothy Nearm, Artistic Director, directed by Melia Bensussen).

A workshop at Jumu Kahua Theater (Harry Wong III, Artistic Director) was in March 2000:

KRISIT .... Jo Pruden
LULU .... Kristine Altwies
PETER .... Walter Eckles
Director .... Mark Lutwak

KRISIT was produced in New York by Primary Stages, Casey Childs, Artistic Director. It opened on 27 January 2001 with the following cast and creative contributors:

KRISIT .... Scotty Bloch
LULU .... Jessica Stone*
PETER .... Larry Pine

*Tracey A Leigh *replaced* Ms Stone *and completed the run*

Director .... Melia Bensussen
Set design .... James Noone
Costume design .... Claudia Stephens
Sound design .... Charles T Brastow
Casting .... Stephanie Klapper
Production manager .... Joshua Helman
Stage manager .... Linda Carol Young
Props .... The Propper Ms Plass

Acknowlegments: For some people some extra thanks: Eric Ray Anderson, Scotty Bloch, Lori Larsen, Tracy Leigh, Jeff Steitzer, and Leslie Swackhamer.

CHARACTERS & SETTING

KRISIT, *female, seventy-five, grand, petty, witty, self-centered, recluse*

LULU, *female, thirty-three, ambitious, smart*

PETER, *male, fifty, self-important, cunning, in the midst of a mid-life crisis and career slump*

Time: Hollywood

Places: a grand bathtub in a grand bathroom.
A table in a grand bar.

Disclaimer: they aren't naked; they're wearing naked suits.

ACT ONE

Scene One

(KRISIT *in a grand bathtub in a grand bathroom. An exasperated* LULU *attends her.*)

KRISIT: *(Deep sigh)* Ah.

(Brief pause. KRISIT *and* LULU *both sniff.)*

KRISIT: *(Disingenuous)* Do you smell pee?

LULU: Soap.

KRISIT: Under the soap!

LULU: Under?

KRISIT: Sniff the toilet.

LULU: It's *fine.*

KRISIT: I suppose you think it's me.

LULU: No no.

KRISIT: That's why you've got me soaking like some soiled undergarment.

LULU: I just thought—

KRISIT: Throw in a little Clorox, why don't you?

LULU: —it might relax you.

KRISIT: My kidneys are failing.

LULU: Your kidneys are fine.

KRISIT: Urine seeping out of my skin. Just like George— *(Beat)* George whatsits before he died. What was his name?

LULU: I don't know—

KRISIT: Bad false teeth, good toupee, always drunk— you've seen him.

LULU: Who—?

KRISIT: Everybody's favorite matinee idol. Love scenes—my God—pee smell seeping through his skin.

LULU: Maybe you peed in the tub.

KRISIT: Didn't didn't didn't.

LULU: It was just a suggestion—

KRISIT: I didn't pee, I *leaked*. Peeing is *active*, and I assure you, this is entirely passive. A spill. Exxon Valdez. Which is why I don't *take a bath*. I take a *shower*. A fast, quick, no-pee-in-the-tub shower.

LULU: I thought it would be a nice change.

KRISIT: It'll be thrilling when you have to call the fire department.

LULU: I'll get you out, Krisit.

KRISIT: Like some puppy stranded in a tree.

LULU: Kitten.

KRISIT: Smelling like pee.

LULU: It's good for your skin.

KRISIT: No, they'd be selling it on T V.

LULU: Next time pee before you get in.

KRISIT: *Next* time? There shouldn't even be a *this* time.

LULU: You're not emptying your bladder fully—

KRISIT: It refilled.

LULU: Talk to your doctor.

KRISIT: What's my doctor got to do with anything?

LULU: He can give you a little stretch down there so—

KRISIT: Ouch ouch ouch.

LULU: —so there's nothing left in your bladder to leak out in the tub.

KRISIT: I can't even think of that.

LULU: I'm sure he won't hurt you.

KRISIT: Like he didn't hurt me Monday? "This won't hurt, dear." Then let me flatten *your* tits between two sheets of Plexiglas, mister.

LULU: Millions of women—

KRISIT: "We have to make it as flat as possible, dear."

LULU: You were fine.

KRISIT: Well I didn't fall into a coma, if that's what you mean. When will this soaking be over?

LULU: When you're relaxed. Do you want to watch a video?

KRISIT: *(Hopeful)* Did you get me Peter's movie?

LULU: It isn't out yet.

KRISIT: I saw the review.

LULU: It's still in the theatres.

KRISIT: What difference does that make?

LULU: You can't rent it when it's still playing.

KRISIT: Buy it.

LULU: You can't *buy* it until you can *rent* it.

KRISIT: I don't want to wait.

LULU: Probably just a few weeks.

KRISIT: I have to wait weeks?

LULU: It isn't even any good.

KRISIT: You saw it?

LULU: Last week.

KRISIT: It just opened yesterday.

LULU: *(Scuffle)* Free— *Pre*— pre—free screening. Free. A friend is a studio…receptionist! Everybody hated it. Bad bad.

KRISIT: Everybody's a critic.

LULU: Not just me. You saw the review.

KRISIT: I don't go by a review.

LULU: Go by this one. It sucks.

KRISIT: Nobody shoots actors like Peter.

LULU: He made exactly two great movies— probably by accident.

KRISIT: He's a *genius*.

LULU: *(Brief pause)* Is Peter…some old friend of yours?

KRISIT: *(Equivocating)* I admire his work.

LULU: Why?

KRISIT: The camera angles, the lighting—everyone is beautiful in a Peter film.

LULU: Maybe Peter has lost his touch.

KRISIT: …You know him?

LULU: No. Of course I don't know him. How would I know him?

KRISIT: Then don't call him Peter like you know him, like you're old buddies, like you've had sex.

LULU: I was just—

KRISIT: I hate that—you watch a movie, you think you get to call the director Peter.

LULU: I was calling him Peter because you were calling him Peter.

KRISIT: Don't call him anything. Don't talk about him. You don't know what you're saying. How many movies have you made?

LULU: *(Scuffle)* I haven't— No. I don't—I *dust!*

KRISIT: Dust, exactly. Leave the movie analysis to the experts. *(Without losing a beat)* You should have seen his first film.

LULU: I have—

KRISIT: *Naked Indifference.* He caressed the actors with the camera.

LULU: *(Prying)* You don't have any of his movies.

KRISIT: I have *all* of them. Locked up.

LULU: ...Did— did you ever work with him?

KRISIT: Never.

LULU: ...Boy, I'll bet he regrets that...that he didn't get to work with you. Boy, I'll bet it's a really big regret—

KRISIT: *(To end this discussion)* Hand me my robe.

LULU: No! You have to soak—let me brush your hair.

KRISIT: My—no! Can't you see it's *done?!*

LULU: Oh, I didn't see—

KRISIT: I did a fabulous job. Don't you think it's a fabulous job?

LULU: Yes, fabulous. It looks like it's been *done.* Did—

KRISIT: Look in the back, look.

LULU: So smooth. Anyway—

KRISIT: Isn't that professional?

LULU: Yes. I don't know how you can even reach back there. Do—?

KRISIT: Yoga. I can stretch, I can bend, I can reach my hair.

LULU: My! I wonder what he's going to do next.

KRISIT: Who?

LULU: Peter. The best thing to do when your movie bombs is to get right back on the horse and make a new one. *(Beat)* I read that. You should call him up.

KRISIT: Why?

LULU: Sure, you could tell him how much you admire *Naked Indifference.* Can you imagine how that would bolster his hurt feelings and cracked ego? To get a call from the great Krisit?

KRISIT: I don't do calling up.

LULU: He'd be so grateful.

KRISIT: I don't bolster egos. Not another word about it. Calling up.

(LULU makes a big sigh, then covers her mouth to hide the mistake.)

KRISIT: …What? Exhausted already? The day has barely begun.

LULU: I'm not exhausted.

KRISIT: Then don't make exhausted sighs. If the job is too much for you, dear—

LULU: No, no. It's fine.

KRISIT: I don't like indiscriminate sighing.

LULU: I know you don't.

KRISIT: You don't know; I'm telling you.

LULU: I didn't come here unprepared. I knew about no sighing.

KRISIT: How did you know?

LULU: I studied your file. It was a slip. I didn't mean to sigh.

KRISIT: What file?

LULU: At the employment agency. I read it all the way through. Twice.

KRISIT: That can't be legal, a file.

LULU: *(Scuffle)* Oh, it's fine, a file. Really fine.

KRISIT: And just anyone can go, and go, and sit and read my *file*?

LULU: …It's so the domestic can fulfill your every whim and desire and need. How else can I know how to serve—

KRISIT: My whim? You think my needs are whims?

LULU: No no, your needs are needs, only your whims are whims—

KRISIT: Harry Bendell has a *file* on me!

LULU: Harry is not going to make it public.

KRISIT: You call him *Harry*?

LULU: Sure, we've had sex.

KRISIT: What?!

LULU: No—I'm kidding—I *know* Harry. I know him. I work for him. We all call him Harry.

KRISIT: What's *in* my file?

LULU: Uh, nice. Nice things. *(Opens paper, trying to change subject)* You want me to clip anything?

KRISIT: Clip?

LULU: The newspapers.

KRISIT: What are the newspapers doing in here?

LULU: Soaking, relaxing, and clipping.

KRISIT: My scrapbook will get all wet.

LULU: No no. You soak and relax, I clip and paste.

KRISIT: Are your hands dry?

LULU: They're dry.

KRISIT: Don't pick up my scrapbook with wet hands.

LULU: They're dry.

KRISIT: Dry them off.

LULU: They aren't wet.

KRISIT: I want to see you dry your hands.

LULU: They're dry they're dry they're dry they're dry.

KRISIT: ...Whatever you say. Do you have the newspaper?

LULU: *(Great control)* Uh huh.

KRISIT: Are your hands dry? *(Little laugh)*

LULU: *(Trying to get a grip)* ...Do you want to see *The Weekly*?

KRISIT: I don't get *The Weekly*.

LULU: I subscribed. It just came.

KRISIT: Hand me *Variety*. *(Derisive) The Weekly*.

(LULU *hands* KRISIT **Variety**. KRISIT *turns the pages.* LULU *takes the* L A Weekly *out of its bag.)*

LULU: Shit.

KRISIT: What?

LULU: Nothing.

KRISIT: You said shit.

LULU: I didn't mean it.

KRISIT: No. You said shit.

LULU: A slip.

KRISIT: Ten days no swearing, all of a sudden a shit? Let me see that. *(She looks at the* Weekly*)* What is it? What? There's nothing ... *(Reads)* "The fifty most important people in Hollywood under thirty-five." Is this why you said shit, this list?

LULU: No.

KRISIT: Why did you say shit about this list?

LULU: ...I didn't think it came out until the fall.

KRISIT: Why do you care *at all* about this list? Are you an important person in Hollywood under thirty-five?

LULU: Not important, surprised—

KRISIT: *(Suddenly)* Who *are* you!?

LULU: What?!

KRISIT: LuLu, LuLu—that's not the name of a domestic.

LULU: Yes it is!

KRISIT: My God— Is there a hidden camera?

LULU: No. Just a LuLu.

KRISIT: I'm not dressed properly—

LULU: What—?

KRISIT: Get me a lip gloss!

LULU: There's no—

KRISIT: Are you my entertainment spy?

LULU: No.

KRISIT: Sent here for some spying purpose?

LULU: *(With finality)* I am no spy. There is no spy. You have no spy.

(Brief pause)

KRISIT: *(Momentarily disappointed)* I thought you were a spy.

LULU: No.

KRISIT: You and your file. ...Give me *Variety*. I wouldn't say shit about a list in the *L A Weekly*.

LULU: It was a mistake.

KRISIT: I wouldn't say shit unless the list was in *Variety*.

LULU: *(To change subject)* Oh! Look! What a nice photo.

KRISIT: *(Excited)* Let me see. I would never take a role like that.

LULU: *(Quoting)* "Luminescent portrayal of the dowager."

KRISIT: She probably *auditioned*.

LULU: Everybody auditions now. I read that.

KRISIT: I wouldn't.

LULU: I know you wouldn't.

KRISIT: *(Sarcasm)* How do you know? Is it in my file?

LULU: Because you mention it every day. She won best actress.

KRISIT: As if anybody cares about Cannes.

LULU: "Performance of the decade."

KRISIT: They don't mean it. It's just an excuse to write about the newest youngest prettiest.

LULU: The whole article is about Joanie.

KRISIT: *(Sees another picture, thrilled)* Look at her face.

LULU: It looks great.

KRISIT: It looks like it's been ironed.

LULU: It is a little…tight.

KRISIT: Ironed! Find me her before picture.

LULU: *(Looking through scrapbook)* Before what?

KRISIT: Before ironing.

LULU: You document plastic surgery?

KRISIT: I document pain.

LULU: Then why are they all smiling?

KRISIT: Because that's the only expression possible. They cut and pull and stretch until all that's left is a desperate grin.

LULU: Plastic surgery is completely reasonable. Imperative even.

KRISIT: Oh, the pain, the pain. I will never let a knife touch my face.

LULU: I had my eyes done.

KRISIT: *(Shock bordering on impressed)* You did?

LULU: What about it?

KRISIT: Come closer. *(Examining)* Where are the scars?

LULU: In here. *(Eyebrows)*

KRISIT: Ouch.

LULU: They give you drugs.

KRISIT: How old are you?

LULU: …Twenty-six.

KRISIT: *(Brief pause)* No.

LULU: Why not?

KRISIT: You just aren't. You simply are not.

LULU: Thirty-three.

KRISIT: …Even the help is getting their eyes done.

LULU: …Harry…

KRISIT: What?

LULU: —likes us to look good.

KRISIT: None of his other girls look good.

LULU: It's a new policy. For all the Bendell domestics.

KRISIT: You let them staple your eyelids to get a dusting job?

LULU: Uh—

KRISIT: *(Over)* My God, where will it end?! Never, I'll never do it, never. Snip and nip and tuck and stitch and slice. For some pathetic role in some pathetic movie. "Save me doctor, my forehead skin is blinding me."

LULU: *(Re: Joanie article)* This is not a pathetic role.

KRISIT: Let it go, let it go. Hang on and become a silly old fool held up to ridicule and scorn. Hot flashes driving the lines from your mind and turning your makeup into glop.

(KRISIT puts a washcloth over her eyes and continues to rant. Unseen by her, LULU takes a small bottle from her pocket and sneaks some oil into the tub.)

KRISIT: Nobody cares about the old lady in the movies. Nobody cares about Joanie—they only care about Uma, or Winona, or Julia.

LULU: People care about Joanie—people care about *you*. Nobody's seen you in twenty-five years—they're fascinated—whatever happened to—

KRISIT: Nobody nobody nobody.

LULU: Last night on *Where Are They Now*—

KRISIT: *(Peeks out of cloth)* ...What?

LULU: They computer-generated your face to see what you look like.

KRISIT: How did I look?

LULU: Beautiful.

KRISIT: *(Preening)* Beautiful.

LULU: But not as good as the real thing. I wanted to call them up and say, you're not even close, you have no idea how good—how *beautiful* she looks. How beautiful.

KRISIT: I take care of my skin. I don't think anybody could ever guess my right age.

LULU: You're gorgeous. You don't look a day over sixty.

KRISIT: *(Pause)* Sixty?

LULU: ...Krisit, you're seventy-five.

KRISIT: Sixty? Really?

LULU: You look fabulous.

KRISIT: What's the point of looking fabulous if I look *sixty*?

LULU: You're robust, healthy, you're beautiful. You should show it off in a movie.

KRISIT: Oh yes, a twenty-foot visage of me looking *sixty* playing opposite some beautiful young thing... Oh. *(Deep sniff)* I'm having...I remember...deja vu, deja vu! My life is flashing by.

LULU: What? No.

KRISIT: Yes, yes, goodbye, goodbye...my life is wafting away.

LULU: No goodbye. Come back. Hello. It isn't your life, it's this. *This* is wafting. *(She reveals bath oil. Sniffs the bottle.)*

KRISIT: What is that?

LULU: I don't know...bath oil?

KRISIT: *(Sniffs)* Something—something from long ago.

LULU: I couldn't read the label, smelled good.

KRISIT: ...This is a distant yet familiar smell. Where did you get it?

LULU: Attic. It was all gooey.

KRISIT: What were you doing in the attic?

LULU: Dusting the scrapbooks. And reading them. I couldn't help myself...what a career!

KRISIT: *(Realizes)* ...This is my pre-shoot emulsion.

LULU: Well, it's truly lovely.

KRISIT: All day long I'm going to be thinking about acting. And then this smell will get on my sheets. I'll be acting in my dreams.

LULU: They'll be wonderful dreams.

KRISIT: I don't want acting dreams. I must re-rinse.

LULU: What about "water conservation"?

KRISIT: I want this smell off me.

LULU: "L A is a desert?"

KRISIT: I don't care.

LULU: "Human beings aren't meant to live in a desert."

KRISIT: Stop quoting me.

LULU: "We are water heroes in this house. As long as you're in my employ, you will be a water hero."

KRISIT: *(Brief pause, grandly)* Carolyn brought me that oil.

LULU: *(Encouraging her)* Really?

KRISIT: *(Enjoys the memory)* I never knew where she got it. She made it seem like a trip to Marakesh. Some Arabian prince squeezing quinces to make my bath oil. Rare drops of aromatic precious oils. *(Sniffing deeply)* Just the thing to clear my head before I entered the madness of the set. *(Sigh)*

LULU: Breathe in the aroma. You were ahead of your time, Krisit. Everybody uses aromatherapy now. It's very trendy.

KRISIT: We used to go to chiropractors to be trendy. Leonard swore by his chiropractor. *(Leonard voice)* "That guy can clear a cold by cracking a back."

LULU: Leonard had a chiropractor?

KRISIT: That guy got more starlets to undress.

LULU: *(Aghast)* Leonard did?!

KRISIT: Don't be silly. The chiropractor.

LULU: Chiropractors don't make you undress.

KRISIT: Now you tell me. *(Little laugh, beat)* Wait a minute, wait a minute. Didn't I tell you about the oil baths?

LULU: What? Oh, you might have, something about a bath.

KRISIT: I did tell you. We were talking about Leonard. Your first day. I wouldn't take his call. You were shocked. "Not take a call from Leonard?" You were very interested in Leonard.

LULU: *(Covering)* It was Leonard *himself*. It was not a second-in-command stand-in. It was *the* Leonard. Leonard is not a man whose fingers dial numbers.

KRISIT: You've had sex with him, too?

LULU: *(Aghast)* Good God—I mean, no. *(Calms down)* I just mean, he, he is not the type of famous person who makes his own calls.

KRISIT: What an annoying man. He was always after me for one ridiculous project or another.

LULU: *(Incredulous)* You turned him down?

KRISIT: I couldn't imagine working with Leonard.

LULU: You said "no" to Leonard.

KRISIT: Am I speaking English? Yes, I said no.

LULU: He's a very important producer.

KRISIT: He's a pipsqueak.

LULU: Pipsqueak?! *(Gasps)*

KRISIT: *(Finality)* I remember a pipsqueak. He badgered poor Carolyn for years, begging and begging her to bring me to the phone.

LULU: But she never did.

KRISIT: That's what killed her—protecting me from all the badgerers and bad news people. Anything in the paper that might cause me pain, snip snip. *Variety* appeared like a happy little Swiss cheese.

LULU: She kept out everything good, too.

KRISIT: It wasn't good.

LULU: It was, it is. I heard good on *Where Are They Now*.

KRISIT: I don't want to hear about it.

LULU: It was good. They showed a scene from *September Moon*.

KRISIT: *(Gasp, then horrified)* No no no!

LULU: It's wonderful— *(Foreign accent)* "I'll not stay so small as to fit inside your dream."

KRISIT: Did they quote that nasty review? Is that heinous review on everybody's mind again?

LULU: Nothing heinous.

KRISIT: I *was* acting.

LULU: …What??

KRISIT: That *bitch*.

LULU: Which bitch?

KRISIT: *Maurine* Bitch.

LULU: I don't know her.

KRISIT: They have to leave me alone.

LULU: It's on everybody's ten-best list, *September Moon*, right at the top.

KRISIT: Stop talking about it.

LULU: You don't even have a copy of it.

KRISIT: I don't want to see it.

LULU: It's everybody's favorite.

KRISIT: Don't you dare bring it in this house.

LULU: The acting—the *effects*—it was years ahead of its time. How did they get you over the lake?

KRISIT: I don't know! I don't know a lake. They probably spliced in a lake. I don't know what they did. I never saw it.

LULU: *(Beat, stutters)* You—you saw it.

KRISIT: I never watched it.

LULU: But, Krisit—

KRISIT: Never never never.

LULU: It's your best one.

KRISIT: Get me out of here!

LULU: You *love* to soak in the bathtub!

KRISIT: That's ridiculous.

LULU: You *said* so—in the big *Look* feature. "Soaking is imperative. The skin must soften so that you can scrape it off and reveal the young skin from below."

KRISIT: Scrape it now and you'll reveal the *organs* below.

LULU: …You will soak in tubs again, Krisit.

KRISIT: What are you talking about?

LULU: A movie…it's all coming back to me…. *(Scuffle)* Leonard! Yes, there's this *Leonard* project! Told to me

by my receptionist friend. Yes! That must be why
Leonard was calling! To offer a part to you!

KRISIT: Nonsense.

LULU: Don't make Leonard ...settle for a Joanie.
Leonard himself on the line, begging, begging you to
take the part.

KRISIT: I don't care.

LULU: Yes, that's it—it's clanging in my mind like a
big bell, I'm such a ninny! The Leonard-Joanie Project
should be The Leonard-Krisit Project!

KRISIT: I won't do it.

LULU: *(Tries something else)* The Leonard-Krisit
Project...with *Peter* as the director?

KRISIT: *(Perks up)* Peter as the director?

LULU: That's it! I remember it so clearly now!

KRISIT: ...Why didn't *Peter* call me? If he's to be the
director.

LULU: Um...must be some professional procedural
protocol...thing.

KRISIT: ...Peter doesn't want me.

LULU: Peter is dying for you.

KRISIT: He hasn't seen me.

LULU: You're perfect—

KRISIT: Perfect? Oh yes, this is perfect. And here's a
perfect one of these—and these are definitely perfect!
A perfect bundle of old oldness—I see what you're
doing—

LULU: *(Caught)* No, no I'm not doing that—

KRISIT: —Pawing over my scrapbooks, sneaking old
aromas into my bath, teasing me with the old routine.
Trying to trick me, trying to revive my longings,

but they're dead, dead as rigor mortis, dead as dead things. You, with your boring little life. Seizing on the opportunity to exploit a faded old movie queen. Drag her out into the limelight, just so you can bask in her shadow.

LULU: A movie would be fun.

KRISIT: Fun? To appear in a movie with *teenagers*? Star opposite a *chicken*? Co-star with a *virus*?

LULU: No—human people.

KRISIT: Never never never. Get me my robe.

(Lights shift. The bathtub and KRISIT *go away.* LULU *walks directly from the bathroom into a grand bar, approaches* PETER *at a table.)*

Scene Two

LULU: Hello—

PETER: Huh?

LULU: Peter?

PETER: *(Standing)* Lulu?

LULU: Yes.

PETER: Oh. Please.

(Motions for her to sit, looks around)

LULU: Thank you. I wasn't sure you were you.

PETER: Who else would I be?

LULU: *(Nervous laugh)* I don't know. Thanks for taking the meeting.

PETER: Are you kidding? You used the magic word.

LULU: Krisit?

PETER: No. Leonard.

LULU: But you said you've been thinking about—

PETER: Oh, sure I've been thinking about Krisit. I'm gonna call her, believe me. I am going to call Krisit. Where *is* um—

LULU: Krisit?

PETER: Leonard.

LULU: Oh. No.

PETER: ...Noooo?

LULU: No Leonard.

PETER: No Leonard?

LULU: Just me.

PETER: You?

LULU: Think of me as pre-Leonard.

PETER: Oh. Will you excuse me? *(Starts to exit)*

LULU: What?

PETER: I'm going to get my pre-Peter. You can talk to her.

LULU: I'll have you know I have...complete autonomy.

PETER: I've never heard of you.

LULU: And we're getting a lot of mileage out of that— what are we having? *(Re: pitcher)*

PETER: *We* are not having anything.

LULU: *(Persisting)* I've never seen martinis by the *pitcher*.

PETER: *(Defensive)* Industry standard.

LULU: A *pitcher* is?

PETER: You don't have to *drink* it, a pitcher. *All* of it. It's a so-the-waiter-doesn't-come-back pitcher. It's a we-don't-want-to-be-disturbed pitcher. For Leonard. I thought I'd be talking to *Leonard*.

LULU: You are talking to Leonard. Tell us about your project.

PETER: What? You want me to pre-pitch?

LULU: *(Beat)* Leonard stayed away to protect you—so nobody knows you took a meeting with Leonard.

PETER: Because I took it with you—

LULU: If it's Leonard, instead of me, by this afternoon everybody in L A *knows*. Everybody is waiting for the announcement about the Leonard-Peter project.

(Brief pause, it sinks in for PETER.*)*

LULU: And if it doesn't come…

PETER: The humiliation factor.

*(*PETER *sits, still hesitant.* LULU *sells.)*

LULU: Peter…you are on a select—short…minuscule list…of directors Leonard is talking to. He's being very…very choosy. All he cares about in these, the waning days of his career, is art. He is only interested in making an art-filled film. A *list*-making film. *(She smiles. He's buying it.)* Come on, tell us about your project. Indulge an old man.

PETER: *(Brief pause, clears throat, pitches) Dancing on their Graves* is all *about* art, art art art. And the soul. The soul of the artist. A very…very famous artist, painter, think Picasso. Monumental early career, changes the vocabulary of painting. Fame, fortune. He hits a slump. He can't think, he can't get an idea. He hits the bottle. He slashes his paintings. His wife, his *wife* starts to lose her mind. Claims *she* painted the pictures. He doesn't know what to do. What can he do?! …What can he do… *(Confused, to himself)* What *does* he do? Oh! He seeks comfort in the arms of another woman— beautiful, sensitive—young—athletic—she is the antithesis of art—

LULU: *(Realizing)* Oh—

PETER: *(Over)* She is *authentic.* She leads him out of the valley of the shadow—she shows him the light— jogging!, aerobics. He gets off his duff, out into the world, the world of youth, Karaoke—world-famous painter lip syncing to Martha and the Vandellas. She shows him…the uh…uh…

LULU: Not the skateboard.

PETER: What?!

LULU: The skateboard.

PETER: How do you know about the skateboard?!

LULU: Uh, you said skateboard.

PETER: I didn't say skateboard. I *wouldn't* have said skateboard. Skateboard is the finale. I wouldn't have said it yet.

LULU: I must have read it in the paper.

PETER: *(Panicking)* Read what in the paper? This is my original project.

LULU: Sort of autobiographical?

PETER: All my movies are autobiographical.

LULU: Yes, I must have read something about you and a skateboard in the newspaper.

PETER: They'll print anything.

LULU: Something around your divorce? Did you have a divorce?

PETER: I don't know.

LULU: A busy divorce.

PETER: Complicated.

LULU: *(Interrogation begins)* Your wife wanted your movie royalties.

PETER: You have a very good memory.

LULU: And writing credit.

PETER: Which was absolutely undeserved!

LULU: She claimed she wrote the hits.

PETER: Mad, she'd gone mad—Mad Maud we called her. She was losing her mind. I had to divorce her, I had to escape, find peace, sanity. Thank God for Tracy!

LULU: The one on the skateboard.

PETER: Doing scroogees, yeah. I married Tracy. I divorced Maud.

LULU: *(Brief pause)* Married Tracy. Divorced Maud.

PETER: Salvation.

LULU: Was there any problem with that?

PETER: No, it was simple.

LULU: What about the law?

PETER: Hey, hey, that age thing was absolutely false. I met her at a voting booth, for pete's sake.

LULU: And married her *before* you divorced Maud?

PETER: No, of course not, what are you talking about? That's all I need. Tracy and I are fully legally married.

LULU: What about Maud?

PETER: Fully legally divorced.

LULU: *Did* she end up getting the residuals from *The Secret Keeper*?

PETER: *(Finger wagging)* You've been poking around in that website.

LULU: *(Caught)* Oh, you're right, that must be where I read it. What's your website called again?

PETER: It isn't my website. How can you think it's my website?

LULU: It's very provocative. "It's no coincidence that the hits were written during the Maud years."

PETER: It's Maud's website. I wouldn't say all those terrible things about me. I wouldn't say Maud wrote *The Secret Keeper*.

LULU: That was a *good* film.

PETER: I know. I wrote it.

LULU: But it couldn't have been autobiographical. *You* autobiographical.

PETER: Absolutely *me* autobiographical.

LULU: Very female point-of-view.

PETER: As only a man can.

LULU: Maud didn't give you any notes, or anything?

PETER: I never took notes from Maud. ...Can I confess something?

LULU: Yes yes, absolutely.

PETER: It's why our marriage fell apart. I won't make that mistake again.

LULU: What mistake?

PETER: I should have let Maud sit at the table with the big boys. It might have...flooded that...fire of... frustration burning in her heart, if I'd even seemed to take a note now and again.

LULU: You shut her out.

PETER: All through the writing and filming of *The Secret Keeper*.

LULU: You made her feel useless.

PETER: Unwanted.

LULU: You made her get coffee.

PETER: Lattes.

LULU: Chained her to the copy machine.

PETER: It isn't her fault she keeps saying all those terrible big lies. I pushed her over the edge.

LULU: You're a cad.

PETER: I'll never forgive myself.

LULU: *(Pointedly)* But you *did* write it.

PETER: Every word every camera angle every cut to.

LULU: It's a great movie.

PETER: Thank you.

LULU: We are very happy to be talking with the writer of *The Secret Keeper*.

(LULU extends her hand. PETER shakes it.)

PETER: Hey! *The Secret Keeper* doesn't hold a candle to *Dancing on Their Graves*.

LULU: I'd *love* to read the script.

PETER: *(Brief pause)* You don't need to.

LULU: There *is* a script, isn't there?

PETER: …Absolutely. But I'm telling it to you. You might not get it…if you read it…it's younger. I'm reaching a whole new market. Not that stuffy *old* market, the new market, the market that goes back and back and back to see it over and over and over again. Letting Tracy sit at the table has been *great* for my vision.

LULU: How?

PETER: Tracy is young. If you want to reach them, you have to marry them. You can't invent this stuff. They are very original.

LULU: That's true.

PETER: And *mean*. An important, *new* mean. A *mean* that is tempered with a kind of thoughtlessness. Sort

of a "you're-fucked-my-fault-I'm-sorry-bye-bye".
(Pointedly) You want a mint?

LULU: No, I—

PETER: *(Pointedly)* I quit smoking.

LULU: Tracy?

PETER: Hey, man, I'm listening to Tracy.

LULU: Interesting.

PETER: Health food, no smoking, physical fitness.

LULU: *(Beat)* Did Tracy help out with your latest film—

PETER: Oh, hey, no, don't go there. *(Brief pause)* Can I confess something? Else.

LULU: Absolutely.

PETER: That film was nobody's fault but mine. Nobody's. Timing. Never try to make a movie when you're green, to quote my guru.

LULU: You have a guru?

PETER: He's a genius.

LULU: Uh huh.

PETER: I admit to skepticism. Then he told me my film was a bomb.

LULU: Oh, no. I didn't think it was a bad bomb—I fully liked it.

PETER: No, no, don't say it. It is important that I look at my work honestly. Even though many people, like yourself, fully liked it, I have to recognize that it isn't my best work. Face the truth and grow.

LULU: Is this twelve steps?

PETER: More than twelve. My list alone is more than twelve, and that's just one task.

LULU: Your list of what?

PETER: My list of the people I have wronged. My task—
if I'm to be the great director I am, is to make amends
where I have wronged. I'm making my way down the
list. And it's working.

LULU: How can you tell?

(PETER *plunks a crystal on the table.*)

PETER: *(Introduction)* Lulu? My crystal.

LULU: Oh. How do you do? It's a lovely...blue one?

PETER: Yes. *(Intimate)* It started out *green.* I'm working
toward pink.

LULU: I've heard about this.

PETER: This is very popular.

LULU: A lot of people believe in this.

PETER: *(Confidentially)* The same people who go to the
movies. *Young* people.

LULU: I see.

PETER: Uh huh. *(Picks up crystal)* Green me was
responsible for that bomb.

LULU: How did you get to blue?

PETER: By working my way down the list of the
wronged. Now it's only green when I lapse. I have it
with me all the time. So I can check. I am very careful.
Everything shows up on a crystal.

LULU: The lapses.

PETER: And the progress. Green me directed a
bomb, blue me is amending where I previously was
offending. Pink me will direct a great movie. *(The point)*
I know you'll want to tell Leonard.

LULU: Oh yes.

PETER: Pink will, I assure him, mark the end of this
current, temporary career...dip.

LULU: We'd want you pink. How long do you think it will take?

PETER: As soon as I get to the bottom of the list. Krisit.

LULU: *(Brief pause)* Krisit?

PETER: She's right there.

LULU: *(Brief pause) That's* why you're going to call her? She's on the list of the wronged?

PETER: She's a hard one. And hey, even the easy ones are hard. Just think about it, if you had to call up everybody you'd ever said squat to or did squat to, *negative* squat, it would be a pretty long list, and you're—you're *young.* Imagine if you were forty. At forty, it's an exhausting list.

LULU: Who's—? Oh.

PETER: What?

LULU: Oh, no, nothing. Really.

PETER: What? You don't think I'm forty?

LULU: Yes, I think so.

PETER: How old are you?

LULU: Twenty-six.

(Pause. He doesn't think so.)

PETER: Well. Twenty-six. You can still make the list.

LULU: Which list is that?

PETER: Come on. *The* list. The fifty-most-under-thirty-five list.

LULU: I don't care about that.

PETER: Oh, sure.

LULU: Did you make the list?

PETER: We didn't have the list.

LULU: Sure you did, the list has been around for…

(Brief pause)

PETER: Okay, okay. I'm *fifty*, okay? Fifty fifty fifty. Fifty fifty fifty.Fifty fifty fifty fifty fifty fifty fifty fifty fifty. Fifty.

LULU: You don't look it.

PETER: You don't look twenty-six either.

LULU: Thank you.

PETER: Boy, this town. Everybody always looking for the new best thing, the newest youngest thing. The most important people *under thirty-five*. Nobody notices that maybe you've gotten *better* at what you do, all that fumbling around you did at twenty-five, you can actually do with finesse now that you have some experience, now that you've been around the block a few thousand times.

LULU: Just like actresses.

PETER: Not like actresses at all. *(Derision)* Actresses.

LULU: They get better and better, but every year a new crop of prettier younger ones get all the jobs.

PETER: That's as it should be.

LULU: Pushing the old ones aside.

PETER: We gotta have new talent.

LULU: Tossing the old ones like yesterday's *Variety*.

PETER: People want new faces.

LULU: What about the old faces?

PETER: They don't want them.

LULU: Maybe the old faces have gotten better at what *they* do!

PETER: Who cares?!

LULU: Krisit! She was a *great* actress. An exquisite actress.

PETER: An exquisite *beauty*. She had that amazing hair. Of course, now we can create that in post.

LULU: Were you...close?

PETER: Hey, no! ...Why? What did she say?

LULU: Nothing.

PETER: *(Skeptical)* Uh huh. No. We weren't close. I haven't seen her in years. Years and years and years. I was just starting when she disappeared.

LULU: You weren't just starting.

PETER: Just starting out.

LULU: *Naked Indifference.*

PETER: What about it?

LULU: You directed it.

PETER: I know I directed it.

LULU: You were already on your way.

PETER: I was on my way to the slag heap. Talk about *wronged*. I'm wronged. Krisit's revenge.

LULU: What revenge?

PETER: *(Realizes)* My God. She'll be talking to *you*, then you'll be talking to Leonard. *Leonard* will be on the Krisit team. *Leonard* will reactivate the revenge. I'm dead.

LULU: *(Coaxing)* Leonard is scrupulously fair.

PETER: The nightmare all over again—

LULU: Leonard will always listen to both sides of a rumor.

PETER: I must pay and pay and pay. Peter turns her down and he must pay for all eternity—

LULU: What—?

PETER: *(Over)* —nobody turns her down, not and lives to hold his head up, not and lives to make another film. Fire up the humiliation factor, we will hang him naked from a flagpole and shine flashlights on his weewee all through the night. *(Looks around)* What?

LULU: What did you turn down?

PETER: I hate that, I just hate that. When you can't tell if you're talking or thinking? Don't you hate that? Oh, man, I gotta. *(Checks crystal)* Oh no. *(Breathes deeply, talks to crystal)* I'm not thinking a negative thought, no negative, only good thoughts, good. I mean, who could blame her? Krisit. Having her little revenge.

LULU: *(Coaxing)* Revenge is a nasty business.

PETER: *(Still with crystal)* I deserved everything I got. I was an idiot, a stupid kid. *(Crystal blue again, to LULU)* Yeah. Somebody like Krisit comes on to you, you go, you don't fuss about technicalities.

LULU: Comes on to you?

PETER: I mean she was beautiful, the most beautiful woman I'd ever seen. But I wasn't even thirty; hell, I wasn't even *twenty-six*.

LULU: She *came on* to you?

PETER: She was sitting on a pile of coats. *(Sexy voice)* "I want you to use me, use me."

LULU: Krisit came on to you?

PETER: What? Does she tell it like I came on to her?

LULU: She was vaguer.

PETER: What did I know? I'd never been with a woman older, and Krisit was a *lot* older. I mean, she wasn't old old, but she was old.

LULU: She'd been around.

PETER: She was a fully formed adult.

LULU: You didn't want to make a fool of yourself.

PETER: Biggest mistake of my career.

LULU: Why do you say that?

PETER: How can you even ask that? Didn't my career come screeching to a halt? Nobody would take my call. Krisit had that kind of clout. Everybody loved Krisit.

LULU: It's so hard to imagine Krisit coming on to you.

PETER: Well, a lot of women came on to me.

LULU: No—I mean no—

PETER: In a bedroom full of coats. It would have been so easy. Saved me so much time. But no, I have to run off with young juicy whoever-she-was. Can't wait to get home to pop it to young juicy whoever-she-was. Whoever any of them were, lining up to go home with me—until Krisit destroyed everything. Oh no, they're not lining up to come home with me anymore. They don't even know my name anymore—

LULU: *(Encouraging)* Uh huh.

PETER: *(Over)* There's nowhere to run, nowhere to hide. That's why they call it Hollywood. Maurine Bitch is right there—

LULU: *(Perks up)* Who?

PETER: *(Over)* Right there at my own club, my own country club, "Better luck next time, Peter." Because of Krisit! I mean I couldn't help myself, couldn't keep my big mouth shut! *(To crystal)* But hey, I'm not like that now. I'm not talking to anybody about anybody now.

LULU: What did you—?

PETER: Zip. Silence.

LULU: But—

PETER: Zip!

LULU: *(Brief pause)* Well. Krisit admires your directing. Even if you are no fan of her acting.

PETER: I don't not admire her acting. *September Moon?*

LULU: A great film.

PETER: *(With foreign accent)* "I'll not stay so small as to fit inside your dream."

LULU: *(Hopeful)* You remember the lines?

PETER: *(Explains)* Where Are They Now.

LULU: *(Disappointed)* Right.

PETER: Why did she do it? She was on top of the world. The performance of the decade. Her first real acting and bingo, she's gone.

LULU: She wanted to go out on top.

PETER: She chewed up the screen in *September Moon.*

LULU: Yes.

(Pause. PETER looks at his crystal.)

PETER: Because I would hate to think she quit because of that Maurine review. I would really hate to think that.

LULU: You know, I can't actually remember that Maurine review.

PETER: Savage.

LULU: I'll have to look it up.

PETER: It was a turn-around performance—the role that turns a starlet into an actress. Maurine didn't see it that way. Maurine insisted we were watching an accident, an aging starlet's accidently filmed *hot flashes…*

LULU: Accidently filmed—

PETER: Hot flashes.

(LULU downs her Martini, and pours herself another.)

PETER: Not acting, an accident. Maurine gave all the credit to the director. And then Krisit was gone.

LULU: A coincidence!

PETER: No.

LULU: Absolutely. Who'd quit because of a little bad press? You'd have to be really insecure and sensitive and worried about getting old to quit because of a review.

PETER: Wasn't she?

LULU: No no no. No. She would never let…no. Krisit? She is much too together, too fabulous to… no.

PETER: Never leaving her house fabulous?

LULU: She leaves the house. Appointments…and meetings.

PETER: Oh…How does she fill her days?

LULU: Appointments…meetings, and she's a water hero.

PETER: Uh huh. The press tried and tried. Never got past Carolyn.

LULU: Leonard tried for twenty years to get past Carolyn.

PETER: Well now he can call her up and make an offer.

LULU: I think Krisit is being very very choosy. Who she works with.

PETER: (Pointedly) He should call her up himself. Not have somebody else do it. Then maybe he'd get someplace.

LULU: I told you I have complete autonomy.

PETER: (Same time) Autonomy. I know.

LULU: To green light the project of my choice.

(Pause, as this sinks in for PETER)

LULU: How's the financing going?

PETER: The financing is going great.

LULU: Uh huh.

PETER: There's a lot of interest. All I need is a little seed money.

LULU: We are very interested.

PETER: *(Hopeful)* You and Leonard.

LULU: If there's a part for Krisit.

PETER: *(Pause)* What are we talking about here?

LULU: It sounds to me like we're talking about a little seed money, at the very least.

PETER: Oh. *(Brief pause)* Oh, well, I don't know. Man. Krisit? There's no part.

LULU: The wife's mother. I pulled the breakdowns.

PETER: That's an old lady part. I need old old. And tough. Somebody really tough.

LULU: Who can act.

PETER: Well, that would be alright, but I really need the deterioration.

LULU: And you keep getting facelifts.

PETER: I do?

LULU: Dyed hair, tummy tucks, hair transplants, false teeth, liposuction—

PETER: *(Clutching himself)* How did you know?

LULU: How did I—? The actresses.

PETER: Oh. *(Recovering)* Oh, yeah. They just…every one of them is *repaired.*

LULU: Not Krisit. She looks every day of her age. Seventy-five-years-old old.

PETER: *(Brief pause)* Well, what do you know? Okay. Bring her in. I'll read her.

LULU: No.

PETER: What no?

LULU: No audition.

PETER: Why not?

LULU: What if you don't cast her? The humiliation factor.

PETER: I don't know...

LULU: We could be talking about full financing.

PETER: Full—?!

LULU: Financing, yes, we *are* talking about full financing.

PETER: She's got it! She's the wife's mother. Full finance— *(Picks up his crystal)* Oh no, no no no...

LULU: What—?

PETER: *(To crystal)* I didn't mean it, it was a joke, a slip—I'm gonna make her audition like everybody else.

LULU: Do you want financing or not?

PETER: *(Whispers to LULU)* I slipped into green just from contemplating it. I can't cast her unless she's best.

LULU: *(Extreme disbelief)* Oh, come on.

PETER: I have no choice.

LULU: Well, get a choice.

PETER: I have to get to pink.

LULU: You don't even have seed money.

PETER: I'll get seed money.

LULU: Not from Leonard.

PETER: If Leonard's ready to finance me, other people will, too.

LULU: *(Blurting)* He's not financing you. He's financing Krisit.

PETER: *(Brief pause)* Then why are we talking? Why are we even pre-talking? Let Leonard call Krisit. *(Pause)* Unless— *(Pause, he puts it together)* Unless Krisit wants me. Unless Krisit won't talk to anybody else but me. Ha! *(Brief pause. He smugly crosses his arms.)*

LULU: *(Trying to bring him back to reality)* Financing, Peter.

PETER: *(Still smug)* Bring her in. I'll *audition* her.

LULU: *(Sigh, exasperated with this madman)* How about an interview?

PETER: I can't tell anything from an interview.

LULU: An interview, where she *becomes* the character.

PETER: What kind of interview is that?

LULU: To all the world it will look as if you are merely having a drink. But she will *behave and speak* as the tough *tough* monster in your script.

PETER: And what do I do?

LULU: You watch. Just like an audition.

PETER: Oh. I get it. *(To crystal)* Can I do that? Great. *(To LULU)* Yeah, bring her by. I do the interview, and then I get the financing?

LULU: If you *cast* her you get the financing!

PETER: *(Worried again)* Oh, right. Make sure to tell her what I need.

(PETER looks worriedly at his crystal as the bar, the table, and PETER go away. LULU walks from the bar back into the bathroom.)

Scene Three

(KRISIT *in bathtub*)

KRISIT: Why didn't you give me the phone?

LULU: You wouldn't have—

KRISIT: I'd take a *Peter* call. What else did he say? Did he really say he can't do the project without me?

LULU: I guarantee you he can't do the project without you. You just have to go talk to him. In your tough way.

KRISIT: Why was he talking to you?

LULU: He'll talk to anybody, even a lowly domestic, to get to you. He's been trying for years and years and years.

KRISIT: *(Pleased)* Years and years… *(Becoming grand)* No audition.

LULU: He knows. He doesn't care.

KRISIT: What else did he say?

LULU: *(Scuffling)* Um… Exquisite…beautiful… luminescent! Tough! That's the best part. Your forcefulness. Your strength. Your toughness. Your tough acting. Who but you can act monstrosity?

KRISIT: I didn't think he even liked my work.

LULU: He loves your toughness. He can't wait to see your toughness again.

KRISIT: I didn't think anybody did.

LULU: …You were in fifty movies.

PETER: Because I was beautiful.

LULU: Because you were tough.

PETER: Then why did he turn me down?

LULU: *(Adamant)* He was a young fool to turn you down. He regrets it. Don't think about it.

KRISIT: I had to work with him. When I saw him sitting on that pile of coats I did something I had never ever done. I asked him to use me in his next film.

LULU: *(Brief pause)* You asked him for a job?

KRISIT: He ran out of the room. Some bedroom with a lot of coats, piled on some bed at some party.

LULU: Let me get this straight—you wanted him to use you in a movie?

KRISIT: It was the beginning of the end.

LULU: ...Krisit, you have to give him a chance to put things right. It will be a great beginning of a new beginning.

KRISIT: A new beginning.

LULU: A chance to leave this bathroom behind, take a walk on Rodeo Drive.

KRISIT: Window shopping.

LULU: Shopping shopping.

KRISIT: New clothes.

LULU: You gotta get out there, Krisit. Give the world what it wants.

KRISIT: *(Hopeful)* What does the world want?

LULU: The world wants you.

KRISIT: The world wants me—it wants me.

END OF ACT ONE

ACT TWO

Scene One

(A few days later. The bar. PETER *at a table alone with a pitcher of Martinis and two glasses.* KRISIT *enters, she is galled; the day has not gone as anticipated.* PETER *spits out his drink.)*

KRISIT: You can see me!

PETER: *(Recovering, too loud)* Look at you!

KRISIT: Thank God. I thought I was starring in *The Invisible Man.*

PETER: I can't believe it.

KRISIT: Believe it. Wipe your chin.

PETER: Now I know why you've been secreting yourself away—

KRISIT: *(Corrects his pronunciation)* Se*cre*ting not *se*creting.

PETER: *(Big heart beat)* Ba boom ba boom.

KRISIT: It sounds like some *fluid* leak.

PETER: So the rest of us don't collapse from your magnificence.

KRISIT: I thought I was invisible.

PETER: Visible and magnificent. The *same* magnificent Krisit.

KRISIT: I need to sit.

PETER: Oh, sure, sorry. I thought you'd rather stand.

KRISIT: No, I'd rather sit.

PETER: Sit.

KRISIT: We used to sit. Don't they sit anymore?

PETER: We can sit.

KRISIT: Sometimes we'd stand. If there were no seats. Cocktail parties, bars. *(Picks up pitcher, sniffs, examines, pours for herself)* Did this start out full?

PETER: Well— *(Looks at watch)* Was the limo late?

KRISIT: Not at all.

PETER: Because I told them not to be late.

KRISIT: He wasn't late.

PETER: I said, she's very important, don't be late.

KRISIT: Early even.

PETER: Did you like the limo?

KRISIT: I liked the dark windows.

PETER: I asked for a no smoking.

KRISIT: What's that?

PETER: *(Aren't I considerate)* You have to *ask* for the no smoking. Did they give you a no smoking?

KRISIT: I didn't see any smoking.

PETER: Well, good, because I'd hate to think of you sitting for hours in traffic in a smokey limo.

KRISIT: No traffic.

PETER: You weren't stuck in traffic?

KRISIT: I was buying this outfit.

PETER: You were shopping?

KRISIT: They talked right through me, like I wasn't even there. I had to zip up my own zipper in the back. Thank goodness for Yoga.

PETER: I didn't say to take you shopping.

KRISIT: Moths.

PETER: Moths?

KRISIT: Gaping holes all over my dress.

PETER: …Holes are good.

KRISIT: They didn't used to be good.

PETER: The *new guys* run around in *rags*. As long as that hole—that artful *rip* reveals a great ab.

KRISIT: What's an ab?

PETER: Something you need if you want forty million dollars for a movie. Good abs, good pecs, good glutes. Rosy cheeks. You can't look like you can have a heart attack and die. No wrinkles in the face, no grey hair in the hair.

KRISIT: Your hair is darker than I remember.

PETER: Yeah, it got darker.

KRISIT: That hasn't been my experience.

PETER: I'm a guy.

KRISIT: And *shorter*.

PETER: Well, yeah, the seventies.

KRISIT: And thinner.

PETER: You think it looks *thinner*?

KRISIT: In front.

PETER: It shouldn't look thinner.

KRISIT: Bring your head closer to my eyes. *(She examines, surprise.)* What is this? What's going on in here?

PETER: It's a weave.

KRISIT: Ah, yes. How does it work?

PETER: It's attached. Woven on.

KRISIT: What are these clumps?

PETER: They can't weave it when there's nothing to weave it to.

KRISIT: Ouch.

PETER: I'll say. There's a new thing I'm looking into.

KRISIT: The spray paint?

PETER: No, paint is gone. Toxic. Little gold snaps they drill into your skull. You snap the hair right on.

KRISIT: Oh my God. Get a toupee.

PETER: And leave it by the side of the pool with my towel?

KRISIT: Ouch ouch ouch—

PETER: No, there's no feeling in the skull. Not like in the jaw bone.

KRISIT: You have snaps in your jawbone?

PETER: Screws.

KRISIT: Oh no!

PETER: What? I should get choppers? A plate?

KRISIT: But screws, my God.

PETER: What do you use?

KRISIT: Teeth.

PETER: You still have those?

KRISIT: Yes.

PETER: Let me see. (*He looks in her mouth.*) Teeth aren't that important. You distract them with your hair, they never see your teeth. Forty million dollar hair.

KRISIT: And it doesn't even look good. Mine was only sixty. Plus the tip for taking me without an appointment.

PETER: ...You haven't been having your hair done.

KRISIT: Yes, where I was ever more invisible than I was in the dressing room.

PETER: *(To the world at large)* She was having her hair done, ladies and gentlemen.

KRISIT: Peter, Peter, listen to me, listen.

PETER: What?

KRISIT: I was invisible. She had no opinion about my face.

PETER: Who didn't?

KRISIT: The hairdresser.

PETER: *(Can't believe it)* Oh, come on.

KRISIT: Yes, *none*. She had opinions about the other faces under the other heads of hair, but mine was invisible. *(Pause)* What do you think it means?

(PETER *fears the answer.*)

PETER: Nothing. It means *nothing*.

KRISIT: It means that I have passed some line, crashed beyond some *point* where anyone gives a damn. The point of no return.

PETER: *(Panicky)* There is noooo point like that.

KRISIT: Where no one is looking.

PETER: They're looking—

KRISIT: Where you're old and invisible.

PETER: Stop saying invisible.

KRISIT: *(To herself)* If no one is looking...why should I care what I—

PETER: Oh yeah?! Who's going to give you forty million dollars? You gotta care. You gotta push that point away, push it back.

KRISIT: It's an on-rushing mountain.

PETER: That's why God invented surgeons! Look at this. *(Pulls out waistband)* I got rid of three inches in twenty-five minutes.

KRISIT: Owee, owee.

PETER: No owee.

KRISIT: You let them cut you?

PETER: Fat suck.

KRISIT: Go on a diet.

PETER: I'd never get there on a diet. The standard is too strict.

KRISIT: What standard?

PETER: *Industry* standard. And my wife. My wife has a very strict standard for trimness.

KRISIT: Your wife made you get fat suck?

PETER: She brought around a few friends, a few shirtless friends. She gave me a few pokes in the spare tire. Hey, I'm no idiot.

KRISIT: Who is your wife?

PETER: Tracy. She's new.

KRISIT: What happened to the old one?

PETER: She got old. The new ones want the fat gone yesterday.

KRISIT: Didn't it hurt?

PETER: No. It's just disgusting. The sound. *(Makes a slurpy sucking sound)*

KRISIT: …They make you drink it?

PETER: No! "Drink it"...you don't "drink it". You put
it someplace else. Pecs, upper lip, *abs*...other places.
Or you can bury it. Sleepy Forest has a special section.
Teeny tiny coffin. Lead lined, white enamel. Pink
Chinese brocade cushions. Guaranteed not to leak "for
a thousand years," like anybody's going to check.

KRISIT: *(Appalled and disappointed)* Oh, Peter.

PETER: ..."Oh, Peter?" No "Oh, Peter." *(To put her in her
place)* Maybe we should get on with it.

KRISIT: Oh, Peter.

PETER: You know what I need, don't you?

KRISIT: *(Nodding for a moment, amazed, as it all comes
together for her)* Yes, I do, I do believe I do.

PETER: Okay, then. Action.

KRISIT: ...It's what *I* need.

PETER: What is?

KRISIT: It's what we all need.

PETER: No—

KRISIT: It's what I've needed for two decades.

PETER: I don't think so—

KRISIT: Two decades *and a half.* *(She moves, she is wise,
her wisdom envelops her. She is really talking about herself.)*
You need freedom! You need mental liberation. You
must stop worrying about what everybody else is
thinking about you.

PETER: That's not what I need.

KRISIT: You do. We all do. You have to stop this. Who
are these anonymous thinkers you're living your life to
please? Your face has crashed beyond the point where
anyone cares. So what? Be the see-er instead of the
see-ee. A burden lifted, a mountain I no longer have to
push a rock up. Be free, be free.

PETER: I don't get it.

KRISIT: Don't you see?! We have *assigned* them this power, we have given it over to them. Her shirtless friends?! Don't put up with shirtless friends. No shirt, no service. Your wife pokes your tummy? Tell her no poking allowed, don't lay a hand on me for poking, only stroking.

PETER: Is this it? It isn't very *tough*.

KRISIT: This is it. This is the way. It will only be tough at the beginning. This is our future. Let yourself be bald. Let yourself be grey. Let that chubby tummy hang over your shorts! We are not going to take it anymore. Resist, resist. *(Toasting, happy)* To me!

PETER: *(Brief pause)* Well, that's just not it. That is just Not. It.

KRISIT: It is absolutely it. I can't wait to get home—so I can turn around and go out again. Cheers—

PETER: *(Miserable)* What am I going to tell Tracy? I told her I could pull this off on my own.

KRISIT: And you can.

PETER: *(To himself)* This wouldn't be like the smoking— this I could do *myself*. The smoking she never left my side. She was right there to wrestle them out of my mouth whenever I tried to light up. She glommed onto me like a crustacean on the bottom of a boat, and I quit smoking!

KRISIT: Good for her.

PETER: Tracy knows. Twenty years old and knows.

KRISIT: …Twenty?

PETER: Yep.

KRISIT: Years old.

PETER: It's great.

KRISIT: What do you talk about?

PETER: What to buy…where to eat…what to buy… what to buy… The patch! Yeah! Tracy showed me the light. *(Explanation)* You can't light up in the middle of a deal anymore. In the middle of a deal, you have to leave the table, go outside and stand on the curb with valet parking. One by one, all of a sudden, nobody is smoking anything. Guys putting their hankies up to their noses. "Pardon me, your cigarette smoke is too much for my sinus." You don't want to turn your back on guys like that. You don't want to leave the table for *any* reason, guys like that, you want the patch. Well, Tracy. She knows. She was right there for me…. She's always there. Mornings noons and nights. You gotta have somebody there. In-house. You can't be going out looking for it. Running around. How can I work the next day? No, when I get home, I can't be going out hunting. I got to put it to bed. She's got to rub my back, rub my neck until I fall asleep. I can't be humping all night, somebody waking me up for more. It grows when you get older, stretches, starts to creep toward the knees. Finally I get a shelailleigh that isn't humiliating, and all I want to do with it is sleep… What?

KRISIT: Um…

PETER: Was I talking or was I thinking?

KRISIT: I think you were sleeping.

PETER: No. No sleeping with Tracy around—all that chatter chatter. What *are* all those words she's always stringing together? *(Realizes)* Opinions! They're opinions. She's got so many opinions. I need somebody with fewer opinions. Somebody quieter. Somebody like Maud. Maud's mysterious silence. But at least it was silent silence. I'd wake up in the morning all tangled in her silence. What could she possibly have been thinking? Whatever it is, it's all going to be in her movie, her movie about me. How I am maligned, how I am persona non grata-ed by that ex-woman. *Maud's* making a movie. About us, me, my life, and who is me, who plays me? A T V actor! At least he's buff. Looks pretty hung in that swimsuit, unless that's some bunched-up rag he's jammed in there to make himself look like he has a live dick. *(Brief pause, to* KRISIT*)* What? What did I say?

KRISIT: Live dick.

PETER: I *said* that?! Man. *(Drinks)*

KRISIT: *(Admonishing)* In my day, we were not this *open.*

PETER: Oh yeah, you had privacy.

KRISIT: Taste.

PETER: We don't have that.

KRISIT: *(Lecture)* We were not this outer. We kept things inside. We examined things while they were still *inside.* Silently visit the soul. *(An order)* Silently *without talking* anymore.

PETER: Oh yeah. *(Takes out crystal)* The soul. I visit it. See?

KRISIT: No.

PETER: Hold it.

KRISIT: *(She takes it.)* Is something going to happen?

PETER: I don't know. What color is it?

KRISIT: Looks a little pink.

PETER: No!

KRISIT: Pink.

PETER: Give it to me. *(Takes crystal back, it immediately turns blue, he sighs.)*

KRISIT: *(She looks at it.)* I *prefer* the blue.

PETER: The blue? The blue is cancel the answering service, shut down the office, run away and hide.

KRISIT: Well, maybe you should do just that.

PETER: ...What?

KRISIT: Until you're feeling a little better; I think it's a good idea. *(She gets up to leave.)* A nice little rest someplace.

PETER: Oh sure! Krisit's answer to every little problem—run away and hide.

KRISIT: ...I never ran away.

PETER: You ran away.

KRISIT: I retired.

PETER: It looked like running to me.

KRISIT: I retired while everyone still loved me.

PETER: What about the press?

KRISIT: The press loved me.

PETER: Well, not every single press.

KRISIT: I have no idea what you're talking about.

PETER: Sometimes people run away because of a bad... nasty review.

KRISIT: ...Who would do a thing like that?

PETER: *(Blaming her)* Me! Twenty-four years old. The worst moment of my life. I almost quit! But I came roaring back against the spiteful revenge-minded reviews of *Naked Indifference*— You— *(Wrenching himself back)* no!! *(To crystal)* Not mad, happy happy happy. Ha ha.*(Breathes, recovers his magnanimity)* It was my own fault. I had in my presence the most important...the *best* actress in the world...ready to... *enlighten* me...and what do I do? An idiot, a foolish foolish idiot.

KRISIT: I didn't know you remembered that.

PETER: Oh, I remember. A boy doesn't forget a mistake like that.

KRISIT: You feel you made a mistake?

PETER: I do indeed.

KRISIT: Well, that's some relief.

PETER: I should have stayed on that pile of coats.

KRISIT: We could have made great art.

PETER: Aside from the "great art", and the sheer *joy*, joy of knowing the great Krisit, you wouldn't have told everybody to slam my movie.

KRISIT: ...I didn't tell anybody to slam your movie.

PETER: Oh no, my career was *coincidentally* flattened after that bedroom incident.

KRISIT: I never mentioned your name after that night. To anybody.

PETER: You made the critics slam me!

KRISIT: I never did.

PETER: Then why did they kill *Naked Indifference*?

KRISIT: *Naked Indifference* sucked.

PETER: No one has ever said *Naked Indifference* sucked.

KRISIT: Well, not to you maybe.

PETER: *(Pause)* It really sucked?

KRISIT: Really truly. Nice camera work, though.

PETER: You didn't set me up?

KRISIT: I don't even know what you mean.

PETER: Oh. *(Holds heart, he is moved.)* Oh, oh man. A burden lifted. My heart that was heavy with hate is light. *(Remembers crystal)* Hey! Look! Look at the glow!

Something's going to happen. Oh, Krisit. I am so sorry!
I never never should have done it.

KRISIT: Done what?

PETER: *(To crystal)* But I was filled with such hate.

KRISIT: ...Done what?

PETER: *(Ibid)* Amends, amends—I will never never
waste my time with hate. I will never ever again seek
revenge. Of course I didn't have a crystal back then
to tell me when I mess up. I wouldn't even *talk* to a
Maurine today. Not about somebody else. Not with a
crystal looming over me. *(He remains focused on crystal.)*

KRISIT: *(Coaxing)* Maurine never liked me anyway...

PETER: Like?! Who *did* she like? Was she even capable
of like? Malevolence incorporated. Assassination with
a pen. Murder Ink! But that thing about the hot flashes,
I never should have put that in her head. Cheers.
(Pause. He drinks.) What? What did I say?

KRISIT: *(Great control)* Oh. No more olive.

PETER: Olive—?

KRISIT: Yes, yes. Sort of an olive emergency.

PETER: *(Calling off to waiter)* Hey—hello—

KRISIT: Go get it.

PETER: Krisit. You have to try again. We can work this
out! But I have to see what I need. The crystal!

KRISIT: Get me an olive!

PETER: Are you sure you want more to drink? I mean—

KRISIT: Now!

PETER: Oh. Okay. Olive.

*(PETER exits. KRISIT stands, moves a little like a prize
fighter; noises like those from a wounded elephant come out
of her mouth. He re-enters, he is taken aback.)*

PETER: What are you doing—? Oh! Great, great. Let me sit first. Action.

KRISIT: *(Great control)* Peter...you...you... *(Loses it)* Scum! You manure smear...you residue on my shoe. Is there upright organic matter that is fouler than this?

(PETER nods, thinking she is auditioning. Throughout the following, as KRISIT begins to enjoy extolling his sins, she gains more control and grandeur.)

KRISIT: You... branding iron! Who are you, you you! Some addled bull who has to have his tummy sucked before his young heifer will stroke him down there.

PETER: Whoa!

KRISIT: Snip the eyes, suck the fat, dye the hair, drill the jaw, screw the skull. That's you. Cut dye drill screw. What's next? Monkey gland powder? Penile injections? Cut it open so the surgeon can pump it up with silicone?!!

PETER: Ouch.

KRISIT: What was I thinking? All those years! Watching your films, watching you grow, keeping track of you because you turned me down, interested only in the one who said no, inventing some *artist* behind my humiliation...watching those pathetic rolls of celluloid you foist on the world.

PETER: Ooo.

KRISIT: Pathetic excuse for an artist, for a man. Does he worry about his art? No. All he worries about is "what do they think of my hair?"

PETER: Ooooh.

KRISIT: When I think of the years, the years not leaving my house, because some squat head put a stupid little phrase into a mean woman's mind.

PETER: Ooo.

KRISIT: Not squat head—loathsome drip of yeast infection—greenish bile of a tubercular lung; the puss boil on an old wrinkled ass. You are disease *residue.* (*Triumphant*) And I lance you! I lance you to expulsion!

(*Brief pause*)

PETER: (*Starts to applaud*) Thank you, thank you. I am saved.

KRISIT: What what what?!

PETER: (*Grandly*) We would like to offer you the role of my ex-wife's mother.

KRISIT: What are you saying?!

PETER: In *Dancing on their Graves*. I gotta write down those lines. "Puss boil on an old wrinkled ass!" Yes! That was a great audition. The absolute best one I've seen.

KRISIT: No—

PETER: I know we're not supposed to call it that. I won't say it again. That foul word. Krisit, let me confess.

KRISIT: Don't!

PETER: Yeah. I never thought you were much of an actor. I always thought you were just a beautiful face. But you are great. You are a great actor. That was great.

KRISIT: I wasn't acting.

PETER: Well, you know what? That's okay, too. If you really are an old monster, it will read better in the film. You're hired. I'm gonna call Leonard.

(PETER *exits.* KRISIT *is stunned. The table, bar, and* KRISIT, *go away. The* KRISIT *bathroom comes in.*)

Scene Two

(That night. LULU *is in the bathtub.* KRISIT *enters carrying a video tape.)*

LULU: "There she is, ladies and gentlemen—"

KRISIT: Get out of my bathtub.

LULU: "The winner of the next Cannes Film Festival, best actress in a drama—"

KRISIT: I'll call 9-1-1.

LULU: They're not answering. Where have you been?

KRISIT: Terrorizing the masses.

LULU: Great!

KRISIT: Frightening babies. That's what old monsters do.

LULU: Yes, yes! Tell me what happened.

KRISIT: What do you care? What does anyone care?

LULU: Oh, I care. I care, alright. Didn't Peter tell you—?

KRISIT: Don't mention that name aloud in my bathtub.

LULU: Did he tell you about the project?

KRISIT: Fling the useless old fool into the lions' den.

LULU: *(Getting worried)* Did he blow the deal?

KRISIT: There is no deal.

LULU: What—? No. I got it all worked out.

KRISIT: I know all about you and your little plan and your little list! Most-important-under-thirty-five. You put me on an ice floe to be buried alive. You threw me to the wolves in the forest fire.

LULU: You aren't in the forest fire.

KRISIT: I will never…*never* leave here again.

LULU: No, you have to leave here, you have to. It's my deal.

KRISIT: Is that all you can think of? Your deal! What does it take to close your deal? It doesn't matter who you sacrifice, so long as there is a deal at the end of the tunnel.

LULU: He has to use you!

KRISIT: Oh, he'll *use* me. Take the poor old woman, tease her with her own memories, her own desires, her own tender exposed longings, then throw her down the well to be crushed in an avalanche of ugly reality.

LULU: I'll kill him.

KRISIT: Drowning in the depths of my own empty pool.

LULU: Forget Peter. We don't need Peter. We'll do a movie with somebody else.

KRISIT: Never, never a movie. Never the public humiliation of a movie. Never never—

LULU: Just a little movie.

KRISIT: Don't even say the word *movie*!

LULU: You have to.

KRISIT: You are not a feeling human being.

LULU: I am.

KRISIT: You have no heart.

LULU: I am so.

KRISIT: I am finished. I see the infinite horizon of my infinite...horizon.

LULU: No—not finished. You can't be finished. Everything—all my...everything—you have to—I'll— I'll do something, I'll think up something.

KRISIT: *(Accent)* "I'll not stay so small as to fit inside your dream."

LULU: You're not small, you're big. *He's* small. We'll finish him, we'll finish *Peter*. That creep. He'll never get financing. Not as long as Leonard is alive. And once Leonard is dead, I'll personally blackball him through the end of the twenty-first century. Peter will never say "action" again. Who needs a Peter? He thinks his career is having a little slump. Just wait. He doesn't know from slump. We'll show him slump. Mister Ex-director. Mister Use-ta-be-big. I'll call everybody in Leonard's Rolodex. We'll make him so small he fits inside anybody's dream... he'll fit inside a thimble... *(Realizes)* Hey...hey... "fit inside your—" isn't that?

(KRISIT *smirks.)*

LULU: *(Continued)* What?

KRISIT: Pretty good, huh?

LULU: What's pretty good?

KRISIT: Acting.

LULU: *(Brief pause)* You were acting?

KRISIT: Yes.

LULU: Just now?

KRISIT: Acting. Was I good? *(She puts the video in the V C R.)*

LULU: ...You convinced me.

KRISIT: Yes. I'm good.

LULU: You are. Um—did *Peter* convince you you're good?

KRISIT: *(All innocent)* Peter?

LULU: Did you have a nice time with...Peter?

KRISIT: *(Noncommittal)* Mmmm.

LULU: I was just—it was a joke, the Rolodex. Peter is a great guy.

KRISIT: Yes. Was-I-talking or was-I-thinking Peter is a truly great guy.

LULU: What happened at the meeting?!

KRISIT: Peter went for the phone. I went to look for a brick, or loose rock. But the sidewalk was pristine. I asked the limo driver to give me the tire iron, but he didn't understand and took me for a drive. When we were hopelessly far from the bar, I directed him to Sleepy Forest. By the time we got there I realized how good I was feeling. I went for a walk. I found the liposuction section, and the gravestone of Peter's fat. I said a little prayer over his dead fat, and then the limo driver took me over to Leonard's.

LULU: Leonard's?

KRISIT: Leonard's. I asked him what he thinks of a young woman who would lie her way into my confidence.

LULU: Not me!

KRISIT: Someone who touches his secret Rolodex.

LULU: Nooooo.

KRISIT: Someone who helps herself to my bathtub.

LULU: Leonard made me do it.

KRISIT: Someone who is planning to take over once *Leonard is dead!*

LULU: …I love your work!

KRISIT: You'll never guess what Leonard had on the V C R.

LULU: *September Moon.*

KRISIT: He watches it every day.

LULU: I know.

KRISIT: I made him turn it off.

LULU: Leonard loves *September Moon*.

KRISIT: He loves me in it.

LULU: Did he say anything...about me?

KRISIT: What would he possibly have to say about *you*?

LULU: About the movie I get to produce.

KRISIT: The movie you get to produce if you can get me to be in it?

LULU: That's the one.

KRISIT: Leonard wants to produce it.

LULU: What about me?

KRISIT: Bendell Domestics are always hiring. I could give you a reference.

LULU: But I got it all set up. I got you and Peter to meet.

(Enter PETER.*)*

PETER: Where did you go?

LULU: You have no business in this bathroom!

PETER: You be quiet, you.

LULU: Don't tell me to be quiet, you has-been.

PETER: *(To* LULU*)* You never-were, you never-will-be! *(To* KRISIT*)* I got back to the table, you were gone. I got home, Leonard's voice on my voicemail, "you'll never be pink, you loser."

LULU: How did you get in this house?

PETER: The front door is wide open.

KRISIT: I left it open for Leonard.

LULU: Leonard?!

*(*KRISIT *gets undressed.)*

PETER: *(Gets crystal)* Oh no. Not Leonard. Not yet. Look at this green. *(To crystal)* I'm sorry, I'm sorry, I'm sorry, I'm sorry.

KRISIT: You must be thinking bad thoughts.

PETER: Krisit. Krisit. What are you doing?

KRISIT: *(A striptease)* Ta ta ta, ta ta ta, ta ta ta, ta ta ta ta ta. Ta ta boom, boom, boom boom boom boom boom boom. *(Etc)*

LULU: *(Over)* What *are* you doing?

PETER: Stop it, stop it right now. *(Pause) Please* stop it.

KRISIT: Don't watch if it makes you queasy.

PETER: Hey, not me, Krisit! Don't call me queasy. I am not the least bit queasy. Never me call me queasy because of clothes removal. I love clothes removal. I am not queasy.

KRISIT: You?

LULU: Uh uh.

KRISIT: Good! Move over. *(She gets in the tub.)*

PETER: You are great, Krisit. Naked with the lights on. I couldn't do it.

KRISIT: You can't stay unless you get in the tub.

LULU: No!

PETER: Can I get in with my clothes on?

LULU: No!

KRISIT: I guess not.

(PETER takes off his shoes, etc.)

PETER: Here I come, yeah I am right there, right there, see how I am right there? I'm not going to be an idiot twice.

LULU: She doesn't want to have sex with you!

PETER: She doesn't?

KRISIT: Well, not before I see the goods.

LULU: What are you saying?!

KRISIT: Really, I'm not interested in anything that reaches the knees.

LULU: What—?

KRISIT: Nice tush.

PETER: Oh, thanks. It's new. It's great for sitting in traffic. *(He gets in the tub.)*

KRISIT: Do you think there's room for Leonard?

LULU: Plenty of room for Leonard.

KRISIT: And Maud?

PETER: Maud? My Maud? How's my hair?

KRISIT: Maud is going to write a movie for me. Something about a water hero, I think. An old lady water hero.

LULU: Peter, maybe Maud will want *you* to direct.

PETER: Of course she'll want me to direct.

LULU: And *I* know the perfect production designer. I'll call him.

PETER: Like the old days. She writes, I direct, just like *The Secret Keeper*. The old team—Maud and Peter. She *longs* for me to direct the old-lady-water-hero movie... oh shit. We're divorced.

KRISIT: Yes. Maybe she doesn't long for you to direct it.

PETER: She needs me!

KRISIT: You *do* shoot actors nicely.

PETER: Tell her that. Tell her.

LULU: What about me?

KRISIT: We'll see.

LULU: I made it happen.

KRISIT: Hush now. I'm going to watch a movie. *(She snaps the remote, movie comes on.)*

LULU: I got you out of the house.

KRISIT: Quiet please.

LULU: I got you to meet Peter.

PETER: What's the movie?

KRISIT: *September Moon.*

LULU: I am the brainchild!

KRISIT: Now, now, be still. I want to see how I am in this movie.

PETER: You're great in this movie.

KRISIT: I'll decide that, thank you. *(Pause, relieved sigh)* Ah.

LULU: …Did you—? Oh no.

PETER: *(Looks into tub water)* Did she?

LULU: Don't worry about it. It's good for the skin.

PETER: *(To KRISIT)* Can I?

KRISIT: No!

PETER: *You* did.

KRISIT: It's *my* bathtub. You have to hold it.

(The movie music swells. PETER and LULU anxiously watch KRISIT. KRISIT watches the movie.)

END OF PLAY

www.ingramcontent.com/pod-product-compliance
Lightning Source LLC
Chambersburg PA
CBHW052221090426
42741CB00010B/2626